A Handful of Water

REBECCA GETHIN

INDEPENDENT INNOVATIVE INTERNATIONAL

Published by Cinnamon Press
Meirion House,
Glan yr afon,
Tanygrisiau
Blaenau Ffestiniog,
Gwynedd,
LL41 3SU
www.cinnamonpress.com
The right of Rebecca Gethin to be identified as author of this work
has been asserted by her in accordance with the Copyright,
Designs and Patent Act, 1988. Copyright © 2013 Rebecca Gethin
ISBN: 978-1-907090-76-9

British Library Cataloguing in Publication Data. A CIP record for
this book can be obtained from the British Library.

Designed and typeset in Palatino by Cinnamon Press
Cover from original artwork 'Face in the Lighthouse' by Lydia
Corbett © Lydia Corbett
Cover design by Jan Fortune

Printed in Poland

Cinnamon Press is represented in the UK by Inpress Ltd
www.inpressbooks.co.uk and in Wales by the Welsh Books
Council www.cllc.org.uk

The publisher gratefully acknowledges the support of the Welsh
Books Council

Acknowledgments

Some of these poems (or versions of them) have been previously published by the following magazines: *Acumen, Envoi, Interpreter's House, Orbis, Other Poetry, Poetry Salzburg, Smith's Knoll, Stand, The Island Review, The New Writer, The Poetry Shed, The Reader, The Rialto, The SHOp*. A version of 'Fluent' was previously published in *Otter Country*, Miriam Darlington (editor) (Granta).

My grateful thanks to all my friends in Litmus Poets, Two Rivers Poets, Company of Poets, Poetry Clinic and all fellow-clinicians and to Kate Light, Andy Brown and Jan Fortune. Special thanks to Bill Greenwell for his delicate operating skills and to my husband, Chris, who always reads everything.

Author biography

Rebecca won her first writing competition at the age of ten with an essay on rabbits for the Wharfedale Naturalists' Society. Early precocity was swamped by children, work, the fever of everyday life and she forgot what she had originally wanted to be: 45 years were to pass before she won the Cinnamon Press Novel Writing Award with her first novel, which was published in 2011. Her first poetry collection, *River is the Plural of Rain*, was published by Oversteps Books in 2009. She has worked as a creative writing tutor in a prison and currently works as a freelance creative writing tutor and writer. Rebecca blogs at:
http://rebeccagethin.wordpress.com/

Contents

'No one can step twice into the same river'
Heraclitus

To Chris

A Handful of Water

Keepsakes

But I keep some unanswered letters in a drawer.
Laid flat they look like windows into the homes
of my past. From here in the dark, I stare
between the lines into the lit rooms
of their addresses. Until the words are warmed
by reading, the tones of their handwriting
stay quiet. She said *It will be autumn*
before I'll have time to think of inviting
myself to stay. It took two days to arrive
with a second-class stamp. By then I'd heard
she'd died the night before. My father wrote the word
love several times, knowing he'd never survive
without it. I imagine him writing my name and address
licking the flap, pressing it firm with a kiss.

Loom

From Rathlin, blades of light
make the dark darker
swinging across the water
to penetrate as far as the stripes
of Kintyre or the flashes
of Islay – a pin-point
geometry to plot
and calculate distances.
Probing the thickness
of weathers, they splice ropes
of signals to moor boats
to the safekeeping of darkness.
And I keep watch as if I need
to hold course to what can't be seen.

River Schrödinger

Impossible to keep hold
    of a handful of water

flowing downstream
    or to isolate its particles

a wave of light
    a swirl of bubbles

The river lies still
    while the waters break apart

merge together
    hydrogen and oxygen

molecules scattering
    and gathering

in a welter of currents
    that pour themselves away

The river holds still
    impossible to distinguish

between what is
    and what might have been

Fluent

Summer rain has fattened the river,
the waters alert, dark as a holt.

Down the race currents gather,
jostling each other to merge

in the pool below. Under-tensions
wrinkle the surface. A ripple firms

into a jink of fur, undulates
into a clay-coloured pelt.

Purpose flows from whiskers
to the tip of a straight-ruddered tail

as he rides the undertow, steers through
the backwash, burrows the depths.

Nightfall

Sometimes you slip into focus
as if a wisp of you took form
in a chink of time where you fall

out of sleep and wake into being a person
watching how the mountain peers at itself
in the tensioned water of a falling tide

how darkness flows into the estuary
in the currents of mountain streams
diluting its silver light to pewter

sea-birds glitter the sandbanks
daylight disintegrates into fragments
just as you re-integrate into what can't have been

Without

In small places – elbow joints,
finger nails; in narrow angles
between eye and lid,
or philtrum and mouth;
under my skin
in aorta, viscera, bronchi,
there lie traits
that happened to coalesce
into me, growing older,
yet still hold the pattern
of what was once you.

Tomboy

She squints at my body to size me up,
flings out cloth I haven't chosen,
smoothes it flat across the table,
thumbing pins along the paper pattern.

With long scissors she slices
down the length, prises sleeves,
bodice, skirt from the fabric,
stitches seam to seam, pushes me

up on the table to twizzle round so that,
pins between lips, she can adjust the hem
till it hangs straight and decent,
the final touch to make me fit.

Fleeting

I walked through the woods today to see
bluebells in flower, before beech leaves mesh overhead.
I'd show you the coppery dimpsey and maybe
flush a glimpse of the deer as they pronk away
with barely a rustle. I'd present you
with armfuls of bluebells and ask if you agree
with my theory that we might not notice the deer
if they didn't kick up their white rumps as they flee.
You have to know where to look so
I'd need to go with you. I've never been there
when you were telling me something
unexplained while listening to the bee-filled air.
You missed the bluebells and the deer again today
but then you've never made it here in May.

All at Sea

i.m John Hasemore 1893-1916

Knowing which day he was to die
he sent a card home that read
I am quite well.

In the abattoir
they shot him at 4.25am –
no one guessed who fired blanks.

The court martial transcript
was written in pencil as if to render him
more easily erased.

A witness reported him shouting
I will not fucking
soldier in France.

He was roped to the limber
of the field gun dragged by horses.
Lacking an officer friend

he defended himself, saying
I have been at sea all my life
and can speak German, Spanish, Italian.

Ten Forms of Cell-shock

i
Sol says he's lost one tooth
for each of the seven years
he's spent locked up, but he still
has all his wisdom teeth –
he wonders if he should pull them out.

ii
Monday afternoon – eyes sunken
skin grey, yawning, not talking.
One man leans on the wall, waiting
for break-time to pass. Wind
hurtles round the prison's chicanes.

iii
Sometimes
behind their voices
I hear mothers
calling their sons
home.

iv
I look up from my work into Mahumud's eyes
at the other end of the table. He smirks
and asks, *What made you look at me just then?*
I shrug. He says,
I was willing you to.

v
The pale old man says
that to get sweet revenge
he switches kitchen orders
so those who josh him too much
only get to eat what they most hate.

vi

When Neil worked in a zoo
the tigers made a noise through their teeth
like this – *fuff-fuff* – as they followed him
round their compound. He raises his arms
above his head and I see the soft flesh is striped.

vii

Alex weeps, sitting with his head in his arms.
Once he smiled because he liked my beads.
He has to close his eyes in nature programmes
just when the prey is caught. He has written
the name he wants to be – *Sophie* –
many times on his book.

viii

A hot day, so the open fire exit lets in some air.
Someone shouts *Get away from there.*
Later, Frank says in an undertone,
All I saw was rows of houses, fields
but, my God, there really is a world out there.
I haven't seen anything like it for months.

ix

A taxi waits at the granite gate
to whisk him, ticket in hand,
to the station. He leaves prison today
but his DNA and fingerprints
are held, waiting to draw him back,
and back.

x

Jackdaws' eyes follow you
across the yards: they look right at you,
pecking over your thoughts.
Eye movements, gestures,
under surveillance.

Sentence

He arrives full of the story he wants to tell.
The thought of getting it out in the open

makes him smile but when he holds a pen,
his mouth tilts as if he might be sick –

with all that he wants to explain to the world
about when things began to go wrong,

that he never meant to grow
into his father's expression.

He's been making notes, line
after line running through his head.

Now it's a chance to write about this
but sentences are difficult to form,

punctuation marks won't stay put
and the tense keeps sliding round the page.

On J Wing, Poetry

He lets me pore over his words,
ask if he means what I think,
tease apart the pauses

in his lines, the tense
while he looks down
at what my finger points to,

sitting close enough for him
to smell the soil I was digging
in the garden the day before

see, in my questions,
the windows I look through;
his radar sensing me softly,

making me wonder
what lies hidden, crouching inside,
for him to be here for so long

just as, until some switch
flicked,
his victim can't have known.

Tribunal

He had no words for what grew between
him and his father down in the garden shed
with its smells of stored apples, potatoes in a sack.
Intent on the objects they were mending on the bench
they passed pliers or chisel one to the other –
large, furrowed hand – soft, marked hand –
a blackbird singing outside, spiders weaving webs,
and cabbages growing in soil they kept hoed,
while the feeling in his vitals formed into shape,
recognised itself, crystallised into the *No*
he said to the recruiting officer at the desk
in the town square. At the tribunal they asked his age –
You're not old enough to have a conscience,
next case, next case.

Letters Home: 1917

Copperplate writing,
slanting right, in a rush to reach
the end of the line.

Brown ink on pages
torn from an exercise book –
pleasantries at first,

mention of snowstorms,
without giving away their
work of national importance –

the entrenching of the *Conchies' Path*
through the quagmire
leading over open moor

to nowhere. He writes of a riverside
near home where trees bend over.
Still, there's talk (no rule of silence here)

the war will be over soon.

-hurst, -burton, -ton under Lyme, -ford

Ash turning ashen

    withering heart

        on rain-darkening twigs

            loosening hold

scattering

    in autumn gustings

        settling on

            accepting earth

their spines and ribs rotting

    into soil with nothing

        in the offing –

            depending or pending –

            next spring

        a thicketing of roots

     burrowing deeper

   rooting out meanings

from earthing of grammar

    translating itself

        into mourning

            into prints on snowing

Old Layde Church

Without so much as a saint's name
the ruin hunkers down
beside the cliff-edge,

peers across the strait
to Scotland's coastline
shining like herring scales.

A round hole through the centre
of the cross with no arms
admits a beam of light

over the graveyard,
magnifying the bruises
of lichen blooming across

the lettering, the furring of moss.
An ear to the hole senses
paw steps, the trickle of the burn –

punctuations moving
through grass, syllables
crumbling under rain,

whatever it was
the dead stowed here
might have prayed for.

Landfall in Co. Donegal: 1826

He treasured what he brought back to his treeless Thoraigh
from the big island off the coast,
where their boat fetched up in the storm.

From time to time he fingered its smooth surface,
the knobbly cup; when no one was looking
sniffed it, recalled the texture of the trunk

its bulges and ridges, the fissures;
the gush of wind in the branches
spiralling down the leaves,

their dazzle of copper and gold,
how he'd scuffed them with his feet.
In his pocket, he sensed the potential of oak tree

taking root, feared to plant it because
he didn't want his secrets growing through the leaves
scattered over the ground.

Hartland

i Houselight: 1810

At nightfall she turns up the wick, stoops to light
a spill at the fire, nurses the flame to the window
where her oil lamp glows all night
to warn passing ships that rocks lie close.
At watch, she cups her hand to stare far
beyond her own reflection in the pane.
To starboard, glimpsing her light
through a spy glass, unless blotted by rain,
ships' masters calculate how tight
to reef the shrouds. When wind blows onshore
they'll need every crewman's strength to haul the sheets
if *Blessing* or *Speedwell* are to anchor
around the Point in its sheltered bay.
Her one speck of star might give them leeway.

ii Lighthouse 2010

The dark stiffens, clouds
      curdle in the churn of light.
 Now, and now, the glare exposes
       furrowed strata in the cliff face,
in the strobe far below
      surf creeps onto the rocks.
Out to sea, the whips of each beam
      thrash through the wall of fog,
where an orange spark
      answers from Lundy.
The lantern flings a line
      through the dark of the wrecked
and the drowned,
      their prayers fizzling out in spray.

Smugglers' Path

Along the corkscrew path to the top of *White Nothe*
I was focussing hard on my feet, step over step
to avoid seeing the slithery drop
                            with no handhold
to the sea breaking on the bone-white rocks
beneath the over-hang.
                        On the last hairpin bend
I saw the girl who had once been me
                                pausing first
to gauge the strength of the wind, a collie at her heels.
That wind was blamming in my ears
                            the swirl and swish
of the long grass made me giddy
                            but she pressed on downhill.

I wanted to call after her
                        that I knew
what was written in the letter she was waiting for;
that I had lived this far,
                        that she'd keep coming back
because we can't stop doing what we fear;
                                and to myself
that this was the same crumbly cliff with its tightrope path
that we were balancing along...
                        only it isn't.

Rathlin Island

By day, the dot-to-dot of lights can't be seen
from Kintyre or Islay, light in their eyes;

while sheep pick their way on stick-thin legs
between spiral-horned skulls of their own, wind tugging

the roots of their fleece, and the still-hunter heron in its cloak
of water watches for pin-pricks of movement;

while hares track the signals of footsteps from the grasses,
their eyes black as bog-water, ears the pink of sorrel,

and the kelp flips over in the waves, a seal nosing the surface,
the dark in its eyes, bent-back hawthorns stand like masts

beside the ruins, their roofs long gone – the faint morse
from those who left on the famine ship, or survived

the slaughter hiding in caves under the cliffs,
guarded by all they knew of the sea, plotting
the course of Arcturus, Regulus, Orion above the world.

Barn Swallows

Fiddlers of the sky outpouring
the quick running lilt of their flight
through their heart-red throats.

I watch their twirling across marshy reeds
sprinkling the fields with laughter –
dark filaments flittering like bats

in and out through slits of another world,
passing initiative from one to another
like a baton they can't hold for long

before flying full throttle through the gap
of a rusted shed window left on the latch
for a hosepipe to fit through.

Stag oak

In the brakes there's a herd
of trees – tined twigs
pale as antlers in the dimpsey.

On heart-beat feet
they nimble between last year's
fallen leaves.

Ears like shadows twitch
as a gust brings down
a moult of leaf husks.

A pile of spent bracken
the held breath of a tawny pelt,
a hair's breadth away

from the globed smoke
of dandelion seed heads
by the thicket.

The owl-moon opens its eye.

Rhinogydd – A Threshold

Flesh of peat and marsh, with skin of moss,
a pelt of reed; spine and ribs knuckled

by ice and rain; dips and hollows
pooled with black water, the blood of rock.

And voices in the wind –
gasps of laughter, sobbing:

a tussock of spiked reeds shakes
like a quiver in a throat

where a spring bursts from the bog,
thrashes downhill over bone-white stones.

Wind fret thuds like calls
from creatures underground –

throatless, without flesh;
sightless – no voice.

The path weaves and twists
past strewn burial chambers,

dusk rising from the hollows,
and a night-blue feather lying on the raw

ground, sucking at weight – under
each tread, the mud oozing

absence, absence.

Choughs

Just as I reach the tip of Pen-y-Cil
where Bardsey appears like a phantom
of rock, a screech pierces the wind.

Three crows are pecking between stones,
their beaks hammering the thin turf.
Not a bird of prey in sight.

In the grey light my eyes are battened
on the narrow path, the drop to the sea.
A gust of crows spirals above,

their wing-tips spread like fingers.
Landing close by, their toes stretch
to clasp the bare ground, legs and beaks

dipped in the blood of their screech.

Three Churches

St Hywyn's Church, Aberdaron

Inside, there's space enough for the many to wait
for the weather to turn so boats can sail for Bardsey:

the graveyard tilts towards the shore of Hell Bay
as if a vessel, over-laden, is listing.

On the beach, sea-birds promenade and wheel
among the stones flocking at the water's edge,

like hopeful pilgrims, knee-deep in the surf;
one for every saint that was never buried here.

St Nectan's Church, Hartland

In the anchorage of the church yard
ranks of gravestones, lit by yellow lichens,
list like boats beached at low tide

pegged with invisible guys to the mast
of the tower that peers through swirling gulls
over murderous rocks, towards the open sea.

St Raphael's, Huccaby

doubled as a school during the week. Scratchy nibs
pinched between smudged fingers speckled
the desk tops with ink. In winter, a log smouldered
in the hearth, smoke rising like a child's breath.

Nowadays they fill the inkwells with primroses, violets –
pollen speckles the wood. In winter, snowdrops
blizzard the churchyard: after the thaw, they gutter out
like embers of children, chilled to their bones.

A Disappearing

i. Snipe

A low mist skulks where land frays into bog –
sedge, sphagnum. My boot unsucks

and the vibration of my footfall
snaps open a springe with a whirr

as the sheen of wet earth tears itself from the ground,
stretches itself into arrowed wings,

mottled by peat and cloud-reflecting water,
unleashing itself into air, letting marsh light dazzle free

and something of myself I hadn't recognised till now
hurtles away, uttering my own sharp cry.

ii. Snipe Drumming

We sit on a mat of bracken at nightfall
and listen together. In whispers we try
to agree on the words that begin to describe
the sound of his tail feathers – not *drumming*,
a breath being drawn across a hollow reed,
like a goat bleating, perhaps a thrum? We strain
our eyes in the dark to see the dive. A gust
of wind can mask it – but there it goes: the voice
of the marsh humming to itself, thinking aloud.

Port

Miles back, a signpost still points the way
but nothing says why the houses drifted

into ruins, foundered at the road's dead end.
Dry stone walls, built by hands roughened

with cold, toss in the swell of the landscape,
its bones picked clean, where they tilled

what Atlantic storm left in its wake: sheep
in the outfields, potatoes in the infields.

They gathered dulse; caught ling or mackerel;
dangled off the cliff for gulls' eggs or flesh;

extracted lamp oil from livers of sharks –
made their living from edges.

Out to sea lies a tumble of stacks,
every outcrop named for its history.

Seamen, intimate with weather fronts,
with rocks and currents, the meanings

of seabirds, called this bay *Port*
for its blessing of headlands, the lucky turn,

the skeletal elbow of quay. Others,
caught in a westerly, called it a curse.

The Old Country

The front door left ajar, as if someone is expected
home – a key on a ledge, a cap on a rusty hook,
a fallen chair. He's followed a bed-time story to look
for his ancestors in their abandoned homestead.
On the table some airmail letters addressed
to Sean in America. He tries to work out the number
of children schooled in the dialect of hunger,
the sacred heart askew on the wall. His face feels pressed
against the breathed-on glass of their past, peering in
on her standing by as, one by one, they packed up their stuff
and kissed her good-bye. He spots a battered biscuit tin.
Running his nails under the rim, it gives with a huff.
Among the dog-eared black and white photos of cousins
is one of himself in school uniform, somewhere far off.

Beneath *Passo della Mezza Luna*

Someone still comes to cut the grass for hay
to feed the mountain goats.
    A wooden rake
    and a shirt on a hook
are left in a stone hut, a cairn.

To fill gaps in the dry-stone wall
round the *Fontana dell'Olmo*
someone has jammed in
    a thigh bone, a scapula,
    a fork's head –
a mosaic of make-do-and-mend.

On the face of cut stones, next to where
the spout of water still arcs
into the drinking trough,
someone has chiselled out
    a sun and a half-moon
    above a human figure
with stick arms, quizzical eyes.

Around the blackened wick of its trunk
    a corona of apples
    smoulders on the turf.
They wrinkle down – spent votives
for the deserted village.

Epilogue

it crouched in his heart
the way the walls he'd built were warm
to his touch
like a woman's skin

the sun on the vine leaves

the scent of fresh dug potatoes

the wind in the chestnut trees
like the sound of rain

and nothing could take it from him
not the unwatched television
they turned on to amuse him

not the sleepless nights
when he kept waking beside
her curved back

Familiar

In sleep I search for the horse – eyes like wood-grain
petal-thin nostrils, a dark tip to each strand of her coat.

I visualise her shut in a stable without food or water.
Without music. Every morning, I would lead her

from the stable to the field with trees for shade. She knelt,
rolled over in the grass and stood to shake herself

before dropping her head to graze. Her yellowy-white teeth
cropped grass with the sound of ripping fabric.

When the horse lay down to rest I lay with her, leaning against
the timpani of her belly, the sound of violins tuning up inside.

One night I dreamed the horse was in the garden.
Jolted awake, I heard little rushes of movement

and stumbling outside, saw the stable door had swung wide,
banging in the wind that keened through the telephone wires.

Spring

Skylarks are nesting inside my clothes.
They fly in all directions out of my pockets,
the whirr of their wing-beats in my ear.

They flicker like specks in the sky
but remain attached to me
by invisible elastic threads,

down which their clockwork voices
vibrate into my sternum
as though I were a lark chick hearing what

I must become – an outpouring
song, luring menace away
from what I hold most dear.

Love of Country

He didn't know what was building
behind the scenes as he groomed the horses,
trod the furrows they ploughed, dug the soil
to grow leeks and spuds, cast seed by hand,
levelled the sights of his twelve bore,
smashed ice with his fist so sheep could drink,
trailed mud into the kitchen on his boots
day after day to his mother's annoyance
so that when soldiers paraded in the street
he hurried to dig trenches, fire shells
and all for the soil that was under
his fingernails, in his skin, ingrained.

Refraction

Even before I knew him he was dead.
Not that he was one to make light

of artillery shells – *flying pigs,*
toffee apples, whizz bangs

and nobody ever thought to ask him
about *Silent Percy*. Someone had to do it

and good at figures, it fell to him,
to quarter the crumpled landscape

through his field-glasses, shielding them
from glinting in the sun

lest a machine-gunner lock on to his position
as he tried to locate the howitzers.

Searching for tell-tale signs:
a column of smoke, sparks, a certain sheen,

the trajectory of fire from which
he calculated co-ordinates, the angles

and range required to aim their jokes
accurately into enemy lines. Back home,

the spicey smell of *Hot Stuff*, the *plop*
of trench mortars weren't the only unsuitable topics.

When I look back at him, as I never did,
I can't make out his bearings … and however much

I thumb the focus to pinpoint his location,
my only constant is his silence.

Playing the Part

i. Under-age: 1915

During training, nobody had explained
the number of devices employed
to kill one another.

He wrote home about the *blackbirds*,
the *unsewing machines*,
the *whizz-bangs* and *pipsqueaks*

When a tame magpie flew into their trench
and seemed to speak German
one of the men wanted to wring its neck.

In his last letter he wrote about the skylarks
that took to the air and began singing
the moment the smoke thinned.

ii. Theatre of War: Nov 11 1918

On the last day – the curtain call:
a German machine-gunner finishes off his ordnance
firing into the air. He steps forwards, removes
his helmet, performs a bow with a flourish
before walking off stage. No leaves are left
to sound their applause.

Somme 2012

Sliding through the dark, stars spark among
the topmost twigs in the wood. A barn owl
shrieks from a tree as if the moon gave tongue,
the creatures of night hunting me down.
Wood anemones glow like bare skin.
If I make a move the owl-moon may flay
the night with its soundless wing-
beats, eyes scanning the ground for prey,
talons poised to strip it to bone.
The landscape is on the alert; it listens
to my tread like a tunneller with his geophone –
first one ear, then the other – calculating distance
and direction as to when my nervous footfall
might land on the unexploded shell.

It's a long way...

i. 'Cabaret Rouge'

Hares settle down to sleep in their scrapes
on the ground, roe deer doze in a copse;
Venus and Jupiter inch apart by degrees,
the bright half-moon makes them fade
as they drop behind the horizon.
The café that stood beside the road
has been flattened – since then,
no clink of coffee cups,
no nips of wine or cognac for a few centimes.
In its place, ranks of white grave stones –
their shadows square-shouldered – not quite
enough light to read the inscriptions:
so many unnamed soldiers,
whereabouts unknown.

ii. Bernafay Wood

Hunching her shoulders, she passes
the old railway station in the wood
where the trees were stricken by shellfire,
the earth cratered and flooded.
Long since abandoned, hazel and birch
now cover the tracks, foxgloves grow
in the sidings. Does she hear a whistle blow,
the hiss of steam? But nowadays, without a fire
in the grate, the station-master's office is chill;
in the waiting room, no rustle of newspapers.
It's summer but even with a jumper and jacket
she feels the cold. Every so often when workmen
dig trenches to lay new pipes or cables,
they unearth soldiers' bones.

Hare

Gusts pummel the moorside
flattening grasses.

A tussock blinks,
veined ears

catch our footsteps,
its heartbeat alert.

Through split-lips
it tastes the cluttered air –

sheep, marsh,
buzzard's shadow.

Wired to leap, back paws
out-pacing the front

leaving a press of stalks and blades,
a furred print in the grit –

a whiplash of thinking
itself into another form.

Badger

As the tide of night reaches the woodland edge,
        spills across the open stretch of field,
tawny owls keen to one another and the moon,
        as if summoned, appears like a creature
marking its territory with animal odour,

its snout whiffling among nettles and docks
        the furred dusk trotting to
and fro at the margin on silent paws,
        its flanks silvery as darkening grasses,
and, alert to night's grunts,
        slurps out the innards.

Night-calls

As I unlock my way out of the prison
        in winter dark,

cries of men hurl themselves
        from the cell windows

like the trash they fling
        into the yard and that's blown

against the mesh. Their voices
        follow me

as though I were alone
        in a gusty subway

stalked by footsteps
        hurrying just behind me.

And every lit window in the town
        is screened against night,

while their throaty catcalls
        curse each other.

Moths, pallid and furred,
        bump and flutter round

the security lights
        yellowing the dark.

La Vallée des Merveilles

the touch of night-blue stone
chills flesh

       thaws in the soundless
blaze of rock

on the sheer face
mottled copper and green skin
smooth as parchment

three eye sockets

from the mouth-slit
a howl   a whine   a sigh

       the longings of men
incised on the rocks

       immersed in their stone love

eyed by wolves

breathing deep while
etching their prayers
in the space between
their thunder gods

conjuring a language
       the wind could not tear from them

forming it
       to draw down the lightning

Filling the Gap

Tangled in the branches of trees, the moon
makes the bedroom bright as the inside

of an ice cube, a violet grid falling across the bed.
Knowing there's room the child slips in to lie against

the warmth of her father's back. On the wall
the shadow of the witch from the gingerbread house

bustles between the stove and the kitchen table
kneading dough, by the look of it,

with her back to the bedroom for the moment.
The witch mustn't know she is watched

and eyelids can't close quickly enough.
Listening to his sleep-breath beside her,

the child feels safe while not being noticed.
The sky closes, extinguishing the dumb-show.

When he rolls over and reaches towards her
she knows it isn't herself he's been missing.

Syntax

She begins to erect scaffolding. The idea
is to connect one heavy
bar to another,
hoisting each one up with her arms.
      She doesn't know
the names of the equipment
but the smell of iron on her hands
                is indelible.
Her fingerbones are stiff.
The attachments keep slipping away,
      falling out
            of her grasp. With nothing
to hang on to, no
roughness for grip, they slide
            off each other.
She can't
erect the framework that she intended
within the meaning:
      it won't hold together.
A question is not
the right tool for an answer. If
she tests it out, putting
      any weight
on the construction,
and it drops
      she will startle
      at the solid clanking.

Nameless

The names we yelled, in the hired coach
taking us to the demo! After, I never intended to feel
as I did – it started as I waited for the bell
to be answered, grew a little more while waiting
for the stick to be dipped in my jar of pee
and change colour. The tea tasted hopeless.
In my hurry I crushed my voice into a tight bundle
and pocketed it, fingering it on my journey home
like an unsigned love-note. The bus was crowded.
Streetlights smeared the window, wipers smoothing
away the rain that spattered the screen,
the glass blurry with thoughts dazzled
in the headlights. The streets where I lived
weren't lit. In the dark I groped around
for a name, but it was already too late.

In a disused game-keeper's hut

A stream dashes past in a deep cleft. From inside,
all she hears is waterfall. Dark as the garden
at night, a mesh covers the grimy window.

No one will guess. She sweeps the dust, runs outside
to gasp. It settles back like things she's heard said.
She pokes feathers she's found into cracks between planks.

Outside, a jay cackles. The woods are as green
and gold as pheasants. There's nowhere else.
For company she borrows a glass bowl, fills it with water,

puts in stones and water weed, scoops up frogspawn
from a pool – the jelly clings to her fingers,
the pulsing specks eye her. Placing this beside

the light she shuts the door behind her, leaving it
exactly as it was. She can't answer what she can't hear.
All that summer the dust leaks must.

In November she shoves the door open to find a bowl
of dried tadpoles – when they slide around
they clink, like small beads.

The Underside

The last time: early summer. She waits at the prison gate.
The drawn-out sense of expectation, the sunshine on the road,
the resolution she'll make him stick to, bus timetable in her hand,
the way she won't ever need to come again, the birds' twitter,
the radio playing somewhere, the things she hasn't thought of,
the advancing car, occupants she fears. He told her not to come.

Another time: like all the others. She waits a long time.
The tannin in the tea, the cardboard cups, the fall from any grace,
babies crying, the rising tide of voices, the surveillance,
shrieks of chairs on floor, what to say, the brave expression,
being herded, the watched clock with slow hands, the five pound
note smuggled from her palm to his, the way his face will fall.

The first time: a wet afternoon. She steps through the prison gate.
The dark passage, signs to follow, the paper clutched in her hand.
The keys of power, the calls of men, the dripping walls,
the no-one speaking, the fear behind her lips, the cigarette smoke,
the keys that lock her in and in and still further in, the long wait,
what he might have meant, *I'm here because of you.*

Kestrel

His anatomy is wind.
Air runs through

the shafts of his coverts;
when he opens his wings

it's as if his own hand
flings up the blade of himself,

bone and sinews flexing
saffron feathers grasp

the tensed muscle
of a head wind:

his dark eyes laser
wind-torn grasses

for trails of mouse urine
or a heart-twitch of vole.

Barometer

i.m. Peter Lanyon, artist (1918-64) who was killed in a flying accident

He grinds up pigments to paint his way out
of his own skeleton. His brush bristles

with nerve endings to catch the feel
of varying pressures. His cells learn

the wind – it's what they long to become.
Re-drawing coastal thermals

into geometries of colour, he loops
gravity into fragile light, releases

perspectives trapped inside. Gliding
through veils of cirrus, he gathers particles,

applies them to his canvas,
and scratches out indentations

with a pointed tool – rust-red cliff
beneath a squall of rain, a shaft

through rock strata looking like muscle,
cartilage. Gouts of oil paint are scraped back

to reveal the underside. In a fold of land
he places a dab of red, a smear of blood –

the roof of a fisherman's house –
beneath all the layers, an anchor point.

The language of shingle

i.m. Harry Miller – late of Rose Cottage

All night in his sleep he's aware of depth,
the heft of water, the suck and drag-back
of shingle – the sea's voice shushed
and gravelly in its larynx of pebbles.

First thing, he reads visibility
of Portland, light on Chesil, clouds out at sea,
wind's designs. Cormorant-eyed he watches
the flash of underwater shoals of herring,
the bass that squirm in the tide like contraband.

When a man falls from the zig-zag smugglers' path
he rows his boat round the headland, knowing
where the tide will have hidden the cadaver,
listening for its long-drawn out Miserere.

The Burning Cliff

*The Burning Cliff on the Dorset coast is so called because in 1815 oil shales
beneath the surface ignited and produced heat and sulphurous smoke for years.*

The edge crumbles; trees lose their roothold
and fall; the graveyard drops into soil,
pebbles, chalk dust. Down below,
slow-moving people are specks
and when you're one of them
it's a slog to keep your feet
on the slide of the wave-punched shingle
the knuckled pebbles drawing you towards
the drag and pull of the running tides,
as the white flames of the sea
seethe in the hearth of the bay,
quenching themselves.

From a ruined kelp burner's house on Rathlin Island

On the shore, rocks are
breathing, muscle
flexing beneath mottled skin.

Between them, shadows rustle,
bristling with salt
in the drying sun. Waves,

heavy with kelp, gasp on the shore –
a sleek brow on a pointed nose
ruckles up glittering.

Basalt chunks grunt
to each other like wavelets
bumping on stone. Water slurps

down the length of a stippled back, flows
into spittled surf.
A mothering rock snorts,

gives a low moan, raises its head
and wallows its tail upwards
into the shape of a boat.

Snout thrown back,
jaws gape into the blood-red savagery
of palate and tongue.

Littoral

On St Columba's Day you can pray at a holy well
       by circling it seven times, dropping
a pebble and a prayer in the water at each pass.

Looking for one, we ask a boatman who sighs,
       Holy wells are springing up all over the place –
we must be getting holier. According to the map

there's one on *Inis Troighe*, an island except at low tide,
       reachable after a scramble down from the quay
to the channel wide enough for a wisp of straw

to sail through – *Bealach an Sloipin.*
       Between stones, the runnel streams into open sea,
red and green fronds tongueing the current.

Hopping across it, we balance and clamber
       over boulders, slither on the jungle
of wrack and wireweed, shining coppery gold in the sun,

their bladders cracking under our boots,
       to the island's sandy beach.
Looking back, we see an old man leading a woman and a boy

along a thin path he knows that crosses the intertidal zones.
       Reaching the other side the grandfather prods
the weeds with a stick. He bends and stoops

to fling them aside like old bedding,
       walks away, turns about, returns to where
he'd first looked. We watch him discover

their prayer-place – a perfect circle in a limestone rock.
       They follow round seven times
as we flounder back to the Way of the Wisp

where the tide has fallen still, winking as if in a well.
       From the throats of stones rises a trickle
of sibilants that swells and flows into plainchant.

No Pretence – 1746

Our paying guest slept with a loaded pistol
beside his pillow – seldom spoke
but understood our Gaelic.

He wore a Highlander's kilt: odd, those bare knees.
All day he watched from a headland,
wrapped in a plaid, gusts whipping his eyes.

We shared the little we had,
warmth of peat, dish of mackerel,
gulls' eggs (but he shook his head at poteen).

Hands white as a dairymaid's –
wore rings on his drawing room fingers
unroughened by farm work or hauling nets.

When a ketch took shelter
he was heard speaking some language
to crewmen who rowed ashore, fetching water.

When wind veered the ship sailed south
and, without a word, he was gone.
Soon after, Mother's scrofulous neck healed.

She remembered how three times
he'd stretched his hand to stroke her shoulder.
She always said she'd been touched by a king.

Stranding

The tide won't take back the death it brought,
its last waves skittering about, as if to fibrillate
its ton of failing heart beat. On shore, the sea,

made flesh, expires. Brought into the air
her sheen dries out. She has been lacerated,
an eye damaged. She can't extend the pleats

of her throat or open wide her mouth to sift krill
to feed herself. She can't breach, arc her back,
spout like a geyser, dive as far as 200 metres.

She once felt infrasonic sounds along her skin,
now water's inner space echoes her silence.
The sea's molecules don't forget their own.

Every night the dark creeps out of the land
floods over the waters; every day the light dies
last in the sea. The stars of Cetus are faint.

Mermaid at Zennor

He thought he heard a woman's voice
call his name in the swoosh of waves,
tasted salt on his cracked lips,
felt her in the tug against his knees
when he waded through spring tide
to haul the boat up the shingle.

At night a form pressed against
his spine. When he woke
to spray splattering the window
she was gone – surf laughing
as she swam back to the sea cave
beneath the thunder.

To bind her to him, he carved
the shape of water in the oak –
the way droplets break apart
and join together, the curve
and curl of wave, the moon drawing
tides up and down the shore.